Speech in an Age of Certainty

poems by

J. Khan

Finishing Line Press
Georgetown, Kentucky

Speech in an Age of Certainty

Copyright © 2021 by Jemshed Khan
ISBN 978-1-64662-521-5 First Edition
All rights reserved under International and Pan-American Copyright Conventions. No part of this book may be reproduced in any manner whatsoever without written permission from the publisher, except in the case of brief quotations embodied in critical articles and reviews.

Many encouraged this chapbook, beginning with my co-conspirators at Inklings: Eve Brackenbury, Maija Devine, Ariel Diaz, Karin Frank, and Cameron Morse; as well, former Kansas Poet Laureate Denise Low, and Mike Harty, Debbie Theiss, Pat Daneman, Lindsey Martin-Bowen, Gene Anne Newcomer, and Helen Hokanson. Of course: Kelly Berry, my lovely muse. Helpful poets at Roderick Bates' *Rat's Ass Review* online forum included Ingrid Brook, Vern Fein, James Fowler Meg Freer, Mare Leonard, Sergio Ortiz, Peggy Turnbull, Robin Wright, and many others. Dan Bohrer produced the cover and accepted nothing in return. The editors and staff at Finishing Line Press were thoroughly professional. Thanks to editors encountered along the way: Rosalyn Spencer at *Rigorous Magazine,* Jonathon Penton at *Unlikely Stories,* Matt Potter at *Pure Slush,* K-B Gressitt at *Writers Resist,* Michael R. Burch at *The Hypertexts,* Brian Daldorph at *Coal City Review,* Maryfrances Wagner, Greg Field, and Gary Lechliter at *I-70 Review,* and Anthony Frame at *Glass: Poets Resist.* Finally, this work is dedicated to the few who direct rational non-partisan speech against power misused: a line which connects John Stuart Mill to MLK.

Publisher: Leah Huete de Maines
Editor: Christen Kincaid
Cover Art: Daniel Bohrer
Author Photo: Jemshed Khan
Cover Design: Daniel Bohrer

Order online: www.finishinglinepress.com
         also available on amazon.com

     Author inquiries and mail orders:
          Finishing Line Press
            PO Box 1626
       Georgetown, Kentucky 40324
              USA

Table of Contents

1. Suburban Stop
2. No-Knock State
3. Modern Blue
4. Suspect Down
5. Chicago Black Site
6. Interrogator
7. Skin in the Game
8. Prison Lingo
9. Invisible Knapsack
10. Maryville
11. Kaw Flood
12. Fracking
13. Flint Hills
14. & We By God Do Claim This Land
16. In a Dark Age
18. Dead Boys
19. #48689
20. Nachtblüte
21. Emperor Hirohito
22. HuRico 2017
23. Head of a Pin
24. Fat Cats
25. Turkey Day USA
26. Speech in an Age of Certainty
28. UK Winter
29. The Colonised (sic) Mind
30. The Tame Swans of Waterbury
31. Slowly They Go
32. Lazarus Force
33. Echolalia
34. Faience

The Suburban Stop

When sirens wail
I close my eyes:
Jesus.
I stop.
I touch my cross—
GET OUTTA the car
when the cop screams *Fu**in' do it now.*
I am one Taser strike from pissing myself,
one chokehold from gone—
buck and wing as best I can.
His baton wrecks my temple,
knocks me sideways:
Jackboots nudge up
against my ribs.
I pray.
My wrists are crisscrossed
behind my back—
I close my eyes:
I wait.

Jesus

The No-Knock State
> *Upon hearing that Barret Brown was jailed (again)*

SWAT teams rumble streets.
Men in black smash down doors.

No one bothered to knock
65,000 times last year:

Hinges ripped from the jamb
with a battering ram or breach grenade.

My friend murmurs,
We live in a Police State—

but I still write and say and read
as I will, as we wait.

He points and whispers,
Someone's listening at the door.

I hiss back, *Surely. Enough. Already.*
Though I turn and look to be sure.

Modern Blue

When he had a paycheck job,
driving was improvisational like jazz or cocktails.
Mostly, this meant never crossing the police presence
that hangs like a blue note over those roads
back and forth from work and home.

The bankers trapped him alive—
bluebloods with insectivorous eyes
and robo-signed appraisals: he signed on the line.
In default: his signature sticks to him like flypaper.
Sheriffs, he says, evict cockroaches like me every day.

Blue as the homeless blues,
he hustles streetside, panhandling
while FDA oils the prescription mill: Fentanyl; Oxycontin; Vicodin.
He offers poison too. Adderal, crack, methamphetamine:
He can be any color he wants except green.

He shelters in the shelters:
City Rescue Mission, Union Homeless Shelter,
in the eaves of underpasses, in a tent between river
and railroad tracks, and bows his head
for Salvation Army breakfast: blueberry pancakes & syrup.

He earned junky veins: shooting-up in the alley.
Jonesing a medical condition.
Blue lights, red lights: flashing. Tweaked and itching.
Scabs tracking hungry veins. Booked and trundled away.
He went cold turkey to the city jail that day.

Suspect Down

Panther lights an unlucky cigarette.
Blue heavens collapse on black.
Witnesses deny he waved a gun,
but the blue line weaves in self-defense.

Shoot to kill. Orders from the Chief.
Citizens blaze & loot the corner store.
Bankers skim the rising tide,
gears whir in the House of Chaos.

Burning buildings cast witchy shadows.
Fukushima trickles down its isotopes.
The evening news hocks a blue loogie.
His momma' hair: a tuned oscillosope.

He was running when shot. Had
more holes than his blood could fill.

Chicago Black Site

imagine us both locked inside
a windowless room with two chairs,

French bread rolls, a case of Cali red,
and a place to shower & shit

surely we would be lovers
even if we spoke untranslatable languages

perhaps you would hum your favorite song,
I would foot-tap a beat.

Our tango would be invisible
except where we touch upon each other,

& wouldn't our bodies inscribe the darkness
with handsweep and tongue.

Instead, one of is hooded & hand cuffed
to a chair in a cinderblock room

with no place to shit.
The other hums Metallica & lights a cigarette

before attaching genital electrodes.
Both rendered invisible

even as the one begins the daily visitation
of small violences upon the body

of the other who wonders:
what precinct is this where police

and suspects alike still root for the Cubs.

Interrogator

When you break me,
and I say this because
I have always felt breakable,
consult your field manual
designed for such situations
by committees of paid ethicists,
jailers, and Psychologists
and dumbed to a sixth grade level
by an otherwise decent
Ivy League MFA graduate.

Pain, hypoxia, ice, fire, or threat
should do the job. Dunk me underwater
and I will not be stoic.
I know my lungs' inward scream,
my brain's struggle with terror
when drowning
for a minute and twenty seconds.

Because suddenly this confession
has come down to my want for air
& I will confess anything you ask
including statements swearing
I was not coerced.
No need to make this difficult.
Look, your superiors already applaud
your work with satisfaction.
Now, where does one sign?

skin in the game

tradewinds
whisper to cold brain—
own anything even dark skin
coffle shackle cracker
coil of rope

hydrocarbons
whisper to fracking brain—
own anything even native skin
DAPL attack-dogs water cannon
icy weather

ambition
ambition occupies skin
whispers to brain—
again and again
everything

Prison Lingo

> *The use of shackles or restraints on pregnant women is common practice in U.S. prisons.*
> —www.wikipedia.org

She's doing *Buck Rogers time.*
    Meaning a long prison sentence

She knows *the four-piece drill.*
    Meaning handcuffs and leg irons shackle her
    to the birthing bed

Her baby will be gone.
    Meaning she's allowed 24 hours
    before her baby's taken
    to foster care and never coming back.
    Adoption and Safe Families Act of 1977
    terminates parental rights of any child
    in foster care 15 of the last 22 months.

Nothing in *Grandma's House*—
    Meaning a prison cell serving as gang headquarters
    where items of value are often traded

no *juice card,*
    i.e., a prisoner's influence or reputation

no *kite,*
    an informational message passed hand to hand

no j*ack mack,*
    canned mackeral used as currency
    or placed in a sock and used as a weapon

no nothing gonna bring baby back.

The Invisible Knapsack
After Peggy McIntosh's essay
"Unpacking the Invisible Knapsack"

We walk into the tail end of the BBQ restaurant rush.
Busboys swoop dirty dishes and wet-rag the counters.
Servers balance hot trays with eyes dead level.
Waiters fast-step and bustle too much to look our way.
We stand at the hostess station trying to seem visible.

Wait Here to be Seated
The Hostess Will Be Right With You.

We share glances, wondering if it's this busy for everyone
—*because you are black and I am white?*
You casually survey the scene wanting to turn and leave
—*the old crow ruffles and whispers: Not Welcome Here*
Perhaps we are being too sensitive
—*how long is long enough?*
You shrug shoulders and look to me
—*like I should know because I have superpowers?*
I pull the trusty decoder ring from my knapsack:
The one I found in a Cracker Jack box that says:
-f-o-u-r-
-m-i-n-u-t-e-s -
-f-e-e-l-s-
-l-i-k-e-
-f-o-u-r-
-h-u-n-d-r-e-d
-y-e-a-r-s-
Then the white hostess with bouncy hair whisks us back
straight as the crow flies to the last side booth—
the one nearest the galley and clashing silverware
—*the one that takes us both back again*

Maryville High School, 1973

> *Raymond Gunn: a 27-year-old African American man torched by a white mob in Maryville, Missouri, USA, January 12, 1931.*
> —*Wikipedia.com*

Our neighbor Stokes spits across the fence,
calls us *A-rabs with dirty petrodollars.*
I don't say anything
because a half mile north of here, back in '31,
townsfolk with rope and gasoline,
marched Raymond Gunn to the schoolhouse.
A man wearing a red coat set the fire—
locally known, never named, never tried.

In school most kids leave me alone.
I avoid Ronny Hecker who badgers me
in sing-song gibberish
while his circling friends smile and smirk.

What scares me is trouble from the Smith boys:
brothers who locked a piglet with the runs
in Joe Lempert's gymnasium locker.
For Show-and-Tell they bring a Mason jar
with Raymond's dark finger: severed, charred.

At our ten-year high school reunion,
Ron buys me a beer at the Dew Drop Inn.
I'm sorry, he says, *I learned racism
at home from dad.* We shake hands, bear hug.
I crook an arm across his shoulder: *Ron,
you never creeped me out like them Smith boys.*

We brag about our high school pranks, the girls
we knew, the cars wrecked. About the Smiths,
Ron says, *They're doing life for murder one.*

Kaw Flood

Spring skies turn gunmetal and the Rockies melt:
waters surge into Big Blue, Solomon, and Saline,
crest and whelm the muddy Kaw,
roil the floodplain with a thousand dramas.

A coyote den suddenly goes under—
pups and parents sucked into the churn.
Squirrels, rats, and field-mice scamper on flotsam.
Carcasses bob and roll and buzz with flies.

The smell bloats the air. Water flushes
a factory farm, washes out holding ponds
and fecal sludge. The Kaw mucks Wyandotte County,
sweeps topsoil, breaches sandbags:

sloshes the West Bottoms and dunks the main Boulevard,
rushing yellow and furious across the last
edge of Kansas on a mad torrent
as if there is never enough time to reach the Missouri.

Fracking

> "Lithosphere." Def. Rigid, rocky outer layer of the Earth consisting of the crust.
> —https://www.britannica.com

be with me
when senses wake
to the bed's

shaking frame,
the ground rumbling
underfoot

as a fault line
slips and widens up
to swallow us,

as needles twitch
on the Richter scale
at the shifting

between
tectonic plates:
we could shout,

*No fracking
in the lithosphere!*
or just lie

in bed and say,
*While it lasted, the sex
was great.*

either way,
we're burning down
our last cigarette.

Flint Hills, Kansas

Snowmelt scours the Rockies until the creeks flash.
Gravel and sand wash into Beaver Creek and the Solomon River.
Cows are calving as water sweeps the land.
The jet stream drops from the north like a Cheyenne raid—
rain slams the high plains, rivers churn,
spring calves stumble into the drowning snarl
that roars the Smoky Hills.

Anvil-grey thunderheads rumble the Flint Hills.
Thirty million bison roamed the tall grass prairie
before General Sherman's final solution to the Indian problem–
kill, skin, and sell until the buffalo is exterminated.
They shoot them down on foot, horseback, and from trains:
the hides are stacked, hacked, carcasses left to rot—
to starve out the Pawnee and Osage tribes.

Now, bison bones still wash into angry creeks
with mastodon teeth, arrowheads, deer antlers.
The surly boneyard river reminds whose land this was.
Barbed-wire fences bristle and glint in slanting rain,
Angus, Herefords, and yearlings graze on wet bluestem grass.
The drenched bovines munch ancient fodder,
the white settlers keep Sunday clean.
Soon the calves—fattened under the summer sun—
move to feed lots and holding pens.
When the box chute opens to the kill floor
the cows will know the bison's fate: *kill, skin, sell.*

And We by God Do Claim This Land

Ye Mayflower's packed: pilgrims, adventurers, sheep and
goats: cannons, artillery & gunpowder stored below.
She skims west across ye faire Atlantic until trew
to September, windes bluster, waves batter, smash upon
ye decks. Gales crack ye maine beam midship, she nigh turns
back. Mr. John Howland washes overboard, nearly dies.

Weekes at sea, weake from scurvie, and who shall die?
Her caulking leaks. We're shivering wett, little food, and
skin turns bloody, teeth fall out. Breath turns
labored and hurt anchors in our bones. Downe below,
passengers & crew affix a great iron jackscrew upon
ye splintering Mayflower beam. Now she sails trew.

Knotted rope & hourglass keep our charting trew.
Without sextant, stars, and compass we would die.
We aime for Hudson's River, but a storme's fast upon
us and we drift north. We spy land at last, Cap Codd, and
helm south along ye coast, but she scrapes hard below,
nearly wrecks on shoals, in rip tide seas we turn.

We saile her back, round Cap Codd Hook after a day, turn
into harbor. Mayflower shall winter here. Trew,
ye arctic wails, timbers groan, a newborn cries below.
By grace of God, neither Susanna White nor baby die.
We christen ye childe *Peregrine*, meaning raptor, and
gather round this son yt God doth smile upon.

Winter corners us here. Provision's slim. Chill upon
our souls. We drop ancor and wait ye sun's return.
The mood grows foule: arguments, mutinous speeches, and
biting cold swirl ye ship. No man finds another trew.
For generall good we agree to lawes & acts, yt less may die:
We fashion ye Mayflower compact, our names scribed below.

Our shallop's in disrepair so a few jump in ye water below.
We wade to shore, find maize stubble, then come upon
seede corn in a mound, buried alongside an Indean yt died.
We take colored beans from a Wampanoag house, and return
to shipp. Six months later we repay ye debt because we are trew.
By now halfe our colonie's dyed of scurvie & buried in New-england.

But by ye harvest season our pilfered seede returns thousandfould from our fields. A pox fell upon ye Indians, trew, they by thousands died, and we by God do claim this land.

In a Dark Age

1.
The man
with box cutters
slices the cockpit door.
Blood spills.

Captain
and wingman
fall to floor.

Bloodied hands
kamikaze
the Captain's stick.

The pilot
banks East to prey,
zeroing towards

what looms high
under Western sky.
He mumbles

medieval words,
remembers circling
a black cube:

A blaze
ignites the shrine
of his brain.

2.
And then: dark forms
burn under blue sky.
Our fabled towers

laid to rubble—
heaped like cairns
upon our dead.

The ash of Holy War
billows like a tempest
through our streets.

3.
We stagger back
to our long-swords
and sorcery:

We haft
and flash wicked edges—
keen as shrapnel.

Drums beat
the readying spell.
We close our prayer circle—
summon the Pentagon,

demand
boots across
the water.

4.
Now
missiles
fall like cudgels
from the sky.
Tank treads
embroider
dusty streets.
Their
hollow shrines
are blazing,
embers
bursting
as a dark age
wakes
to
wicked spell.

Dead Boys
Title and last line after "Dead Girls" by Kim Addonizio

The camera pans hillside jungle,
zooms to our hero,
body splayed, face up
and stubbed by a missing limb.
Next, the signature close up:
angled handsome jawline,
blue eyes snuffed and clueless.

In another film studio,
buddies find their missing brother
on the road to Kandahar. Someone drops
bloodied dogtags in a Ziploc baggie
to be delivered to the house
where he grew up playing *Call of Duty*,
where death was an internet hiccup.

Nothing grips a theater
like a busted-up hero. His platoon's
gonna 'copter what's left of him
to medics who will trundle him
upon a reddening stretcher,
cut & stitch him back to life,
unsever
his arteries unless he dies first.
Who would want to be him?
Any Johnny raised on YouTube

and spaghetti westerns who can pocket
a few Glocks and enough rounds,
strap on some Kevlar. Even plain Joe
who feels he don't amount to much
and likely won't, already convinced
that his kind can't get a fair shake.
Except that he can be that hero,
glittering redeemer of the race
thick in the fusillade of gun and rifle fire,
the special, dead, dead boy.

#48689

She was nearly seventy and catching the evening news
when the buzzcut Skinheads appeared on the big screen TV
gathering to explain that it was all just a hoax.

She had thought the Dead *dead*,
but now the remnant past prickled about her:
the peephole of memory swung open.
Tiny white bones began rising up to consciousness
and she journeyed back into cattle cars,
marched through the fresh and falling snow.
When tilling fields for crops she was startled again
by the tiny white bones of babies turned to fertilizer.
She revisited the half-living about the edge of fire,
and heard voices from her childhood
that had gathered to the chambers.

Now, when I walk in her sewing shop
she looks up and her pale eyes flash and smile.
The bulb of the vintage Singer machine
blazes yellow on the backs of her hands
as her fingers draw thread
through a needle's eye.
Her veins are old, full and blue like tattoos.
When her hand feeds fabric to the seam,
the veins bulge and I see the dull blue numbers
on her forearm are ink from another century.

She tells that a few survived the chambers:
Those bodies that still breathed
were dragged out no differently
and stacked with the dead;
all then doused for the burning.
After the blaze of fuel was spent
and the fiery core had already sunk to ash,
the edge of the smoking heap was mostly char.
Little much survived past that smoldering edge—

Just the upper body still alive
with a hand that moved a bit
and a face tilting upward.
The eyes locked intently upon her,
sharply holding her at witness.

Nachtblüte

Dresden blooms rejoice like birds
of love. They bloom and take flight—
wherever they land: more bright blaze.

Timbered tenements spring to flame,
and Dresden burns and burns—
incinerates on the hot spit of night.

Amid crackle of wood and splinter of beams,
firebombs hem in huddled families alive—
rows and rows of apartments scream.

In the morning as the city smolders
and Allied pilots share cigarettes,
the good Generals down black coffee

and cut the shoulders clean and square—
fire up their best cigars. As for the dead,
they too are smoking in their beds.

Emperor Hirohito

1.
One moment, bright standing as a prophet
before the sun, his Emperors' face ever-turned
to the transit of heaven's bright rayed ornament.

Then sky glints briefly.
A shuddering bleaches to the marrow.
Two cities molt in an instant—each puffs once, sways briefly,
and lets loose long bones and skulls.

2.
The God-Emperor concedes nothing.
He keeps courtly distance: His words recorded
onto a scratchy phonograph for low-fi radio transmission.

Hirohito broadcasts nationwide
in erudite Japanese diction—
rarified beyond common understanding.

Rise like dandelions into this orphaning breeze,
survive, and keep to our ancestral honor.

His somber recorded cadence carries through the radio,
the phonograph needle tics and hisses like a Geiger counter,
reminding all of the terms of surrender.

HurRico 2017

You should help yourself. And plan better too.
Island & hurricane, pina & colada: these go together.

I hear you are still without power, or is it just electricity?
Sorry we have no budget to airlift generators, water, or sat-phones.

The SEALS and Rangers would bring medicine to your village
but they are killing brown people half a world away.

Don't blame FEMA for not thinking this forward:
Who knew Maria would track that way?

Next time, keep some plastic jugs of water and bleach ready.
FEMA likes you better if you lighten up a bit.

Look, responsible citizens booked flights,
corporate jets, yachts too. Those people

got out before landfall. They helped themselves.
They help themselves to everything.

Dancing on the Head of a Pin

In the bang of war
a rifle butt smacks
the sniper's shoulder:
another bullet swifts
the long dark hollow
of the killing barrel.

Minutes after the landing
the Rooster is strutting.
As cameras roll,
handshakes all around,
top brass is beaming,
and cheering begins.

I scarcely fathom the howl
of all this volumed Kevlar—
yet my nation dances
on the bones of the dead
to bend the will of others
to a pin on a map.

Fat Cats

The rescued kittens
Have turned to nasty cats
With pregnant bellies.
Nothing good can come of Fat Cats
Lounging on Lincoln's bed,
Hacking up fur balls.
Pissing cat piss.
Nipping at toes:
These are not sweet kittens
Except by name
As they plot cunning leaps
From the banks
Of the flocked velvet sofa.
Claws readied for the coming.
Hoping for another taste
Like that mouse
that had gone warm
down the gullet
A few moons back—
Leaving nothing
But a whimpering stain
On the neighborhood.

The cats are already crouched
Towards another botched landing
Punctuated by the dull thud of misplaced ambition.
There will be a scramble of claws
And indignant squeals
And then;
Voila! The Fat Cats steady themselves
Before carefully licking the blood
From their paws,
Preening their glossy selves,
And getting back to business
Licking their swollen teats.

Turkey Day USA

Thanksgiving
we came prepared
for a family fight,
our fingertips blackened
by *The Times* or *Wall Street Journal*,
our tongues wetted
by the sloppy liars gracing Fox or CNN.

After thanks,
we sat for dinner
armed with loud truths.
Words shot from our mouths.
Spittle arced the table.
We wiped our faces, emboldened
by what felt like passion.

We wolfed slices of warm flesh
and rounds of beets,
as big-screen people
who don't know hungry
pardoned a turkey
on the White House lawn
because *Symbolism & Theater.*

Network cameras kept feeding
awkward gobbler-scenes
into our living rooms as we argued.
After a tussle over the wishbone,
we all looked up from slop and gravy
and cheered that witless Tom.
Saved, God bless, by the President.

Speech in an Age of Certainty

dark angels
refuel their black wings
at 30,000 feet,

keen to visit
modern havoc upon
a sleeping village.

When they open the bays
40,000 lbs of armaments
fall from fuselage.

Those distant explosions
confirm our nation's radiance.
We swell

with patriotic awe,
let fervor be our virtue
now that stealth

has cloaked
our savage intent
and dimmed our view.

How suddenly
darkness enveloped us.
How quickly

it had enlarged—
silent, untouchable
until it dissolved

every bound
of restraint.
— — —

—No.
I refuse this
blindness.

Clearly

others raised
warning
against
empire & war,

objected
to the calculus
of final solutions

or the slinging
of lynch ropes
over sturdy branches.

Surely there were
objections
to winter blankets
sprinked with pox,

refusals to salute
men with epaulettes
attached like hate
to the uniforms of state.

UK Winter, 1963.
> *Page and monarch, forth they went, forth they went together*
> *through the rude wind's bitter lament and the bitter weather.*
> —Mason Neale, 1853

I set out to school
in a flimsy anorak,

sleet nips,
teeth click in arctic chill.

My breath frosts the invisible,
I tongue-taste snow.

Goose bumps sting.
Feet skirt puddle mix

but slush seeps the insoles,
and toes turn cold.

My socks squish each step
until inside school.

Teacher prays,
Let us hymn the day

> *Good King Wenceslas looked out,*
> *on the Feast of Steven,*
> *When the snow lay round about,*
> *deep and crisp and even.*

Outside the window,
large flakes tumble.

By break time
I am warm, I am King,

white velvets everything.

The Colonised Mind

> *What any colonial system does: impose its tongue*
> *on the subject races.*
> —Ngugi wa Thiong'o, "Decolonising the Mind"

For me, it is already done:
My parents' ghazals shushed and mute;
their language siphoned away
by force of nursery rhyme, church choirs,
by various baptismal schemes.

Colonial garrisons occupy
the language centers of my brain—
my thinking circuits click the Anglo way.
Something was traded for wampum,
Venetian beads, cowrie shells...
my tongue twists but cannot say.

DNA still drives my bones and skin
but I am tongue-tied, beset historically.
Far from nest or clan or den,
my diaspora brain adapts as best it can—
colonised because language can.

The Tame Swans of Waterbury

Passion or conquest, wander where they will,
attend upon them still
             —WB Yeats

The small waterway surrounds an island where swans
sleep on open ground. Each neck and head turned back
and resting along the groove of back and wing.

                Their feathers were trimmed back
in swanling time. They will never fly, but nest and court
and mate by the seasonal clock. It is March. They dunk
their heads and necks in a floating dance. He flat-foots himself
onto her broad back and lifts her neck with his beak
as she sinks.
                  After that awkwardness,
they nuzzle as if posing for calendar shots. For weeks they bicker
over branches and twigs as they build a five-foot-wide nest
with foot-thick walls where she lays her clutch.

    The apartment manager notices, dons her hip waders,
crosses the ornamental stream and rushes the nest. The hissing
cob rises up and beats back with the tough carpal bones of his wings,
but she carries a shield. We hear clamoring wings, knocking bones
and watch from apartment deck as she switches out the pale clutch,
leaves wooden eggs. Commotion subsides. The thief retreats
and the pair returns to tending hatchling dreams.

Slowly They Go

I expected handcuff clicks about the wrists,
eyes red with pepper spray, a haze of tear gas,
cell phone videos capturing troubled days.

Too late I realized the cunning gist
of protests that shimmer on-screen.
Slowly scenes disappear from the net,

first the Neo Nazi's, then the homeless Vets.
Facebook and Google delete the rest.
No bullet, no blindfold, no cigarette.

Lazarus Force

That day over lunch I was going to write about the Yemenites starving while the Saudi's build five new palaces on the Red Sea. A poem might make a difference. But the sun was shining, 75 degrees in October, and the outdoor pool is heated, so I went for a swim instead. As I swam laps I felt joy and splash with each stroke: thankful for clients traveling to see me in their combustion driven vehicles and for cheap fuel that leverages each shiny day. For three laps I considered the convenience of gasoline and writerly leisure. Okay, yes, a Lockheed Martin missile incinerated another Yemeni schoolbus, but how could a lunchtime poem make amends for fifty dead school children or eight million starving?

> *Poetry of angel wings and metrical feet,*
> *I thought you were the steed of change,*
> *that with the right words*
> *we would skywrite the nation's conscience.*
> *Now I see my words never had Lazarus force*
> *and we are no match to the God of gasoline.*

The cardiologist said my heart stopped. The apartment manager says I was pulled blue from the pool: resuscitated with CPR and defibrillator paddles across the chest. I survived the ambulance ride, heart stents, ICU, rehab. Today I put my head back in the game. Read an anthology of resistance poetry. Each work smoldered on the page until my chest burst into flame. I rose from the bed, grabbed my pen, began to write again.

Echolalia

> *somethin' will happen to take*
> *the fear outta your bones an' the sweat off of your eyelids*
> *an' drain them to the sweet winds*
>   —Dolores Kendrick, Hattie on the Block

Head
thrown back,
she hurls
the quivering vowel
of grief.
Her tongue
shrills air.
She is vibrance.

Her voice
flows out and back
again
in a wavering refrain of loss,
an open-mouthed spell.
Her sister joins,
and then an aunt, and women
from where

she
does not know,
they raise a capella of sorrow.
And all the voices you do not know,
they gather their fury in to one.
And then they teach
their young
what it is that we have done.

Faience

Copper steeple, church bell sky.
I am drunk from chalice wine,

pray until stained-glass
God gives another gift:

a red brick from the street.
For the shattering. Heft it.

High windows. Marble steps.
Heave. Smash into shard glints.

Because the moon is my peyote
I will howl tonight.

Sulfur is the color of my eye.

Acknowledgments:

Poems have appeared or are in-press in *I-70 Review, Coal City Review, Fifth Estate, Howl Up To Sky, Unlikely Stories, Rigorous Magazine, Barzakh, Heartland 150, Pure Slush, The Hypertexts, Cockwise Cat,* and *Writers Resist.*

Suburban Stop	(*Rigorous Magazine*)
No-Knock State	(*Writers Resist*)
Modern Blue	(*Howling Up To Sky*)
Suspect Down	
Black Site Chicago	(*Barzakh*)
Interrogator	(*Unlikely Stories*)
Skin in the Game	(*Barzakh*)
Prison Lingo	
Invisible Knapsack	(*Rigorous Magazine*)
Maryville	(*I-70 Review*)
Kaw Floods	(*I-70 Review*)
Fracking	(*Pure Slush*)
Flint Hills	(*Heartland 150*)
& We By God Do Claim This Land	(*The Hypertexts*)
In a Dark Age	(*Rigorous Magazine*)
Dead Boys	(*Rigorous Magazine*)
#48689	(*The Hypertexts*)
Nachtblute	(*Rigorous Magazine*)
HuRico 2017	(*Unlikely Stories*)
Head of a Pin	(*Heartland 150*)
Fat Cats	(*Clockwise Cat*)
Turkey Day	
Speech in an Age of Certainty	(*Unlikely Stories*)
UK Winter	(*Coal City Review*)
The Colonised (sic) Mind	(*Rigorous Magazine*)
The Tame Swans of Waterbury	(*I-70 Review*)
Slowly They Go	(*Fifth Estate*)
Lazarus Force	(*Writers Resist*)
Echolalia	(*Barzakh*)
Faience	

www.ingramcontent.com/pod-product-compliance
Lightning Source LLC
LaVergne TN
LVHW041603070426
835507LV00011B/1293